Dedicated to EWKM...

<u>Unlocking the Digital Rosetta Stone for Gen Xers</u>

Greetings, fellow Gen Xers! Are you tired of feeling like a stranger in the digital wilderness, where abbreviations and emojis have taken over the world of communication? Do you ever wonder if the letters and symbols flying across your screens were invented in a secret Gen Z laboratory, leaving you baffled as you attempt to decode this new language? Well, worry no more because I've got you covered!

Introducing "WTH Does That Mean?!: The Gen Xer's Guide to Gen Z Lingo" - your very own Rosetta Stone for the modern age. In these pages, you will find the keys to the kingdom of youthful conversation, where understanding the acronyms and expressions that make up Gen Z's texting lingo is as essential as knowing where your car keys are. Because honestly, can you even TTYL without this knowledge? Nope, you really can't!

Now, I know what you're thinking. "LOL," "BRB," and "OMG" - they all seem like they belong to some strange, secret code, don't they? But fear not, dear Gen Xers, for this guide will demystify the seemingly cryptic world of Gen Z text-speak. It's time for us to bridge the generational gap, and what better way to do it than by learning their language?

WTH Does That Mean?! is your key to unlocking the enigma of texting acronyms. It's not just a dictionary; it's your secret weapon for connecting with the younger generation. So the next time you encounter an "SMH," you can confidently return with a "LOL." And when you're chatting about an "OOTD" with your Gen Z pals, you'll be able to join in without missing a beat.

In this digital age, understanding the acronyms that define Gen Z culture is as important as knowing how to program your VCR back in the day (and let's face it, you never really figured that out, did you?). So, let's embark on this enlightening journey together, armed with the knowledge that will make you the coolest Gen Xer in the room. "TBH," that's a pretty sweet deal, right?

So, my fellow Gen Xers, grab this guide, put on your finest flannel shirt, and prepare to decode the cryptic messages of the Gen Z universe. Let's embrace the digital age and show the younguns that we, too, can LOL, BRB, and OMG with the best of them. Let the texting adventure begin! ●▮💬

Happy texting,
Jess
P.S. You got this, Gen X! 🤘

1. LOL

Laugh Out Loud

** Be aware. This does not mean Lots of Love and is not an appropriate term to send to someone when they tell you about the death of their beloved pet...!

2. BRB
Be Right Back

3. OMG
Oh My God

4. TTYL
Talk To You Later

5. IDK
I Don't Know

IDK

Best Friends Forever

7. SMH	Shaking My Head
8. BTW	By The Way
9. GTG	Got To Go
10. IMO	In My Opinion

*SMH can also mean: So Much Hate or So Much Help!

11. ROFL

Rolling On the Floor Laughing

12. LMAO	Laughing My Arse Off
13. FYI	For Your Information
14. JK	Just Kidding
15. ICYMI	In Case You Missed It

16. SWAK

Sealed With A Kiss

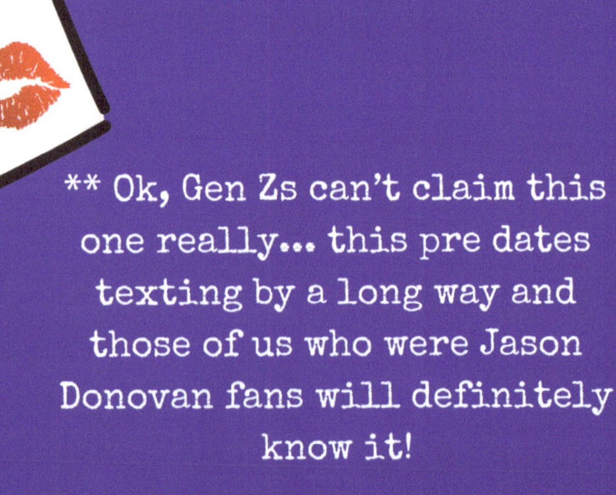

** Ok, Gen Zs can't claim this one really... this pre dates texting by a long way and those of us who were Jason Donovan fans will definitely know it!

24, HBD

Happy Birthday

25. **AFAIK**	As Far As I Know
26. **TBH**	To Be Honest
27. **BRT**	Be Right There
28. **WYD**	What You Doing?
29. **OMW**	On My Way

30. ILY

I Love You

31. SOL	Sooner Or Later
32. BTDT	Been There Done That
33. HTH	Hope This Helps
34. DND	Do Not Disturb

35. BAK

Back At Keyboard

36.	**L8R**	Later
37.	**WFM**	Works For Me
38.	**ICYWW**	In Case You Were Wondering
39.	**IKR**	I Know, Right?!
40.	**NBD**	No Big Deal

41. WTH

What The Hell

42. FFS	For F***'s Sake
43. STFU	Shut The F*** UP
44. WTF	What The F***
45. IDGAF	I Don't Give A F***
46. JFC	Jesus F***ing Christ
47. GTFO	Get The F*** Out
48. NFW	No F***ing Way

ARGH!

49. FML

F*** My Life

*You can also emphasise this phrase by adding an "A" for F*** My Actual Life. Used by exasperated mothers everywhere!

50. TL;DR	Too Long; Didn't Read
51. AYKM	Are You Kidding Me
52. OMDB	Over My Dead Body
53. YOYO	You're On Your Own
54. TIL	Today I learnt
55. LMK	Let Me Know

56. HAGD

Have a Great Day

57. NAGI	Not A Good Idea
58. TTYL	Talk To You Later
59. AYT	Are You There?
60. TYSM	Thank You So Much
61. BOL	Best Of Luck

62. TTFN

Ta Ta For Now

www.ingramcontent.com/pod-product-compliance
Lightning Source LLC
Chambersburg PA
CBHW040901260726

48664CB00024B/422